I'VE BEEN RELEASED!

Being Delivered From Strongholds and Living Your God-given Purpose

I'VE BEEN RELEASED!

Being Delivered From Strongholds and Living Your God-given Purpose

Nieta S. Dortch

Author

All rights reserved © 2018 by Nieta S. Dortch

No part of this book may be reproduced or transmitted in any form or by any means, graphic, electronic, or mechanical, including photocopying, recording, taping, or by any information storage retrieval system, without the written permission of the publisher.

Unless otherwise stated, Scripture is taken from King James Version, which is public domain.

Unless otherwise stated, all definitions taken from source of Webster's Dictionary, published by Merriam-Webster.

Author: Nieta S. Dortch
ISBN-13: 978-0692172032
ISBN-10: 0692172033
LCCN: TBD
Editing: Ty Waller for Young Dreams Publications
Typesetting/Book Cover: Young Dreams Publications

Connect with Nieta S. Dortch

Email: NietaShamoneministries@yahoo.com

Dedication

This book is dedicated to my Lord and Saviour, my King, my Strong Counselor, Jesus Christ. Also to every person whom God called and predestined for His purpose. For God says in Romans 8:30 (KJV), "Moreover whom He did predestinate, them He also called: and whom He called, them He also justified, and whom He did justified, them He also glorified."

To those who believe that you are not fitted for the kingdom because of past mistakes and bad decisions. I pray that my journey will be a testimony for you, to encourage you to launch out so that God can get the glory out of your life.

Be blessed.

Acknowledgments

A special thanks to everyone who encouraged me to stay the course and become all that God has called and created me to be. To my son's father, Demetrius Sr., thank you for speaking life into God's plan for my life and depositing into my purpose. To my one and only child, Demetrius Dortch III (aka Turbo), for being a part of the journey and vision – it is truly breathtaking. God allowed me to see myself through you.

To my Shepard, Pastor John F. Hannah for teaching me how to live a life of abundance - your life is a testimony to me. Thank you for being obedient to your calling, your obedience prepared the path for me. One man's obedience is tied to many destinies.

To all those who said I would not make it and wasn't qualified remember this, God doesn't call those that are qualified, He qualifies those He call. May God bless you and heaven smile upon you.

A special thank you to my patient and kind consultant and editor, Ms. Ty Waller. A special thank you to my New Life Family. To my dear mother, Marlene Sanson, who dedicated her life to God when I was five years old. Thank you, Mom, for always praying for me, and covering and believing in me even when I wanted to give up. You saw past my flesh and spoke to my spirit man.

To my loving God-sent twenty-plus friends Janice, Lisa, Chantelle, Tashema and Wahkeunna you guys rock!!! Thank you for always sticking by my side even when I was unlovable.

A special thank you to my nieces, Torria, Marlene (Wendy), LaQuisha, and my dear, big sister, Michelle for being a part of my journey.

Last but not least, thank you to my Release Dance Family, thank you for hanging in there while I was a work I progress.

Table Of Contents

Introduction

Acknowledgments

Chapters:

1. The Seed
2. The Journey
3. The Vision is Birthed
4. When Man Says No, but God Says Yes
5. When Others Forsake You
6. Encourage Yourself
7. When to Let Go
8. Fight For God's Truth
9. Fulfilling Your God-given Purpose
10. I've Been Released
11. Conclusion

About the Author

Introduction

Have you ever had a burning feeling inside of you? A feeling that you know you're supposed to be making a difference? A feeling that constantly pulls you into believing that you are somebody?

But sometimes that feeling is hidden by the reality of your life. You begin to allow doubt and self-talk to enter in and you tell yourself that you aren't anyone special. That God can't and won't use you because you believe you're a sinner, and you've made too many bad decisions. This type of self-doubt is what the enemy uses as a window to bring in the spirit of doubt, guilt, depression, and ultimately suicide.

The Bible says, "Where there is no vision the people perish because of the lack of knowledge." What is the vision that God has given you? Can you tap into God's word and follow it? When you allow yourself to flow in God's vision, you will see that you're specially created in the image of God and that you were put here for a divine purpose. Then you will have the power to break free from those strongholds that once held you in bondage. You will see how much God loves you. He will adopt you into His kingdom, He will take you in, clean you up, and give you the best. God will reveal your purpose and you, too, will be able to testify that "I've Been Released."

NIETA S. DORTCH

The Seed - Jeremiah 1:5

Chapter One

It was a late October in the year 1988, I was fourteen years old, my mom and I had moved to a part of Chicago known as the "low-end" which was around the housing projects, Stateway Gardens and Robert Taylor homes. During our transition, so many questions entered my mind. Why did we move to the ghetto? Out of all the places we could and should have moved to how did we end up near the projects? What was my mom thinking? Before our move, I had a plethora of friends and went to a great school. For me, life was great, and I wanted it to stay that way! I just could not understand how we ended up in the hood.

My first day at my new school, Wendell Phillips, I remembered entering in with great fear. Upon walking into the school building, I recalled being met with metal detector and police officers. This was cultural shock for me as with my old school I was used to being always greeted each morning by smiling teachers and friendly staff. I was completely out of my comfort zone. My agenda every day was to get to class, do my work and get home as fast as I could. Because of the neighborhood, I prayed daily that I make it to and from school safely without being robbed, shot, beat up, or even raped. All I could hope was for those four years to go by as fast as they could.

      After a few weeks I became settled into my new environment, I found that finding my classes was easy, the students were cool, and the teachers were nice and caring. I thought to myself maybe it's not so bad after all being in a new environment versus my old one. I had a schedule of my classes, and I was excited to get to my favorite of them all, JROTC. I figured this could be an opportunity for me to learn how to protect myself if I needed to. I believed that JROTC would prepare me for the battle that I dreamt in my mind (plus I was scared of water, so no gym for me). Early on I'd made the decision that upon completion of high school I was going straight to the military. I wanted to travel the world and get a good education, become someone, and live the dream that has always been in the inside of me. People often say if you want to make God laugh, tell Him your plan.

I was surprised at how quickly I began to make friends and get familiar with the teachers. It was quite surprising that I was now excited about the school, oppose to how I felt about it when I first attended. After all, Paul says, whatever state you find yourself in we must be content (Philippians 4:11). Things were turning around for me with every passing day. I also eventually joined the fancy drill team. Dancing has always been a passion of mine, and although the drill team wasn't my first choice, it was the closest thing to dance that the school had to offer.

After several weeks I was elevated to being able to help choreograph some of the dance routines, and of course, the art of dance now enters. The students are excited, the teachers are amazed. That day as I walked home I had a big smile on my face, I no longer felt that I was in the ghetto, the world around me was beginning to feel like home.

Fast forward to being well into the school year, and I'm ecstatic to say that the fancy drill team was shutting down every assembly and the popularity of the team caused many more students to join the team. Another fabulous thing happened as well, I was promoted to drill sergeant! I was so excited, and I took my role seriously, nothing was going to stop or distract me! All of my years of living dance has always been my tunnel to channel all my feelings and rough experiences through. Knowing at the end of the tunnel there is light and hope. The more I danced, the more the passion for it grew. Dance soon began to produce some positive fruit in my life.

After having some experience of being drill sergeant I was moved to start my own dance team outside of the school, the Jack A Netts. I felt accomplished as that we excelled to be able to be a part of the Bud Billiken Parade on a yearly basis. This was a rather big deal as this parade would often receive national media attention. We also traveled locally to parties, skating rinks, etc. putting our skills to work. The Jack A Netts grew rapidly. However, there was one problem. Many of our neighborhoods faced restrictions due to strong gang activity. Some of the dancers could not cross certain streets because of where they lived. Some of the dancers felt that they would be opening themselves up to being set up by rival gang members. As the leader, I took it upon myself to help out my team members. I remember bravely talking with some of the gang leaders on behalf of my team. And it also helped that I had a good cordial relationship with most of the gang leaders. They agreed to keep peace as long as we represented the Low-End of Chicago well. Wow, a new level of pressure, but the Bible does say, "He will never put more on you than you can bear." As the art of dance took over, I observed that it captured and became a tunnel not just for me, but for others as well.

Things are looking brighter. I had made some cool friends, the teachers are great, this is not so bad after all. One day I enter into the drill hall, and I see a handsome young guy, watching every move I make. I am thinking is he looking at me? Who does he belong to? I do not want to get into any fights over a boy. He approaches me, and we began to talk (little did I know he was assigned from the enemy to shut the things down God put in me). If I knew then what I know now, my journey would have went differently, but then I wouldn't be able to write this book. But now I know to choose destiny over flesh. As my Shepard would say, "let your mess be your ministry."

This young man and I started a budding relationship. Our sweet talks quickly turned into dates. By the time my sophomore year, I had gotten myself into a world of mess. That handsome young man didn't know his own worth, let alone mine, and was dealing with strongholds in his life. We were two extremely talented teenagers headed down a dark path. I wouldn't have ever thought that this young man will go through with me experiencing two miscarriages, two live births, and one abortion – which I will talk about later. He humiliated me in front of many of my friends and family due to his cheating ways and the cause of two STD contractions. At the age of sixteen, I stopped dreaming and forgot who I was. In spite of it all, I danced through everything because it was the only thing I felt great at doing.

    It's funny how time flies when you are having fun and trying to escape the pressures of life. I am in my fourth year of high school now, and my school is being threatened to be shut down. Attendance has dropped, student grades are at a record low. What happened? This school had started to flourish. I begin to ask myself what could I do to inspire the students to return and keep the school open. I spoke with the principal, teachers, staff. I asked for permission to start a dance group inside the school but not connected to JROTC? I explained how I can ask my former pastor at the time to come speak on behalf of the community and see if he could get the leaders and other officials involved. I asked, and he agreed. Now I was on a mission, I had three months to make a difference.

Wow, the idea was great and successful. Over fifty students joined the dance team, and others were waiting for their test results in classes to be grade eligible to join. My former pastor spoke with other community leaders, and the *save our school assembly* was wonderful. Student attendance was up, grades were improving, and unity was being formed throughout the community. Wow, violence had been semi-replaced with the love of dance. Look at God!!!! His word says in Matthew 19:26, "Jesus said, with men it is impossible, but with God, all things are possible if we believe.

Stronghold: Distraction : noun: A thing that prevents someone from giving full attention to something else. Webster dictionary

Scripture: Luke: 9:42 KJV And as he was yet a coming, the devil threw him down, and tare him, and Jesus rebuked the unclean spirit, and helped the child and delivered him AGAIN to his Father.

Prayer: Father God I ask that you touch every person reading this chapter from the top of their head to the sole of their feet. I bind the spirit of distraction, NOW, in the mighty name of Jesus. Your word says ANYTHING we bind on earth, you, Daddy God will bind in heaven. Spirit of distraction take your hands off the minds of Gods people, NOW, in the mighty name of Jesus. I decree and declare that God's people are being set free from the spirit of distraction and that your people will be healed, delivered, and set totally free from it so that they can do your will in your time so that their God-given purpose can be birthed forth. Amen!

I'VE BEEN RELEASED

The Journey - 2nd Corinthians 5:17

Chapter Two

After such great success, how did I get here? At sixteen years old the most horrific thing happened to me, tragedies hit me hard. By the age of twenty, I went from having two children to burying two children. My first born, Lil' Cody, at five months old had to be hospitalized for four months from contracting an illness. I'll never forget, the day he was supposed to come home he died all alone. The day before his death nurses and doctors assured us that my son was doing better and he would be fine. They encouraged us to go home and rest to prepare for him to come home – we did so trusting in the doctors. Unfortunately, my baby's health quickly took a turn for the worst having liver failure at nine months old.

Two years later we tried again and had a beautiful daughter, her dad, my ex, Cordell thought it was best to name her after me – so here we have Lil' Nieta. It was like I was reliving a nightmare. At seven and a half months she was hospitalized and died a month later. I remember sitting and pretending to be alright, singing our favorite song until she took her last breath. I was told that if I cry out loud that she would transition quicker. That's how I learned to just hold it in regardless of the pain I'm facing. Tears will not change the situation. Trying to be strong for myself and her father. Saints, I don't know which was worse, not being there while your child is dying or sitting there and not being able to do anything to help your dead baby. During this time I was also pregnant with my third child. I think the stress of all that I was experience was the reason I wanted to abort the child. My doctor sent me for a mental evaluation but after a few session,s it was agreed that termination of pregnancy was the best decision for us at the time.

    But I'd find that God doesn't like for you to take life into your own hands. Baby three was strong, and the abortion procedure was a difficult one. Due to complications and large blood loss I died on the table. Even though at the time I wasn't thankful, but I'm grateful now that they were able to revive me. I remember getting out of the hospital angry and upset with God because he brought me back. I would have rather died than go back to that verbal and abusive relationship that was my marriage. The lies and the cheating was taking me out. I was constantly asking God why? Little did I know God still had a plan and He believed in me – even when I didn't believe in myself. But before I got to His plan, I took a path that God never intended – one of pain and disappointment.

After 6 years of being married to my high school sweetheart and enduring being cheated on, lied to, verbally and physically abused, to the point of being knocked out I finally gained the courage leave and divorce him. I remember waking up in Michael Reese Hospital wondering how did I get here? But before me coming to, I heard him whisper to me, "You better not tell anyone what happened. It's all your fault." When I came to, the police asked me what happened? Because a neighbor said, they heard arguing then silence only to find you laying still on the ground with your two-month-old baby a few feet away crying. Oh, I clearly remembered what happened, but knew it was best if I said nothing. The seed that was planted in me where did it go? I use to encourage others to live a good life, now I am ready to take my own.

Several years have passed by, and yet I have learned to stay strong - so I thought. After getting through my divorce with my first husband, I thought I'd met the love of my life. We got married – I thought it would be happily-ever-after. I was living the American dream. We had great jobs, a beautiful home in Westchester, IL. I thought, *OK, I am getting back to me.* However, I never pictured my life without the art of dance being present, but I figured I had moved on to better things. Everything a young married couple could have wanted we had. Now years later, *everything* a young married couple didn't want we had. Debt, marital problems, you name it we experienced it. Then the decision was made, it's time to go our separate ways. Not only did we separate my son was only eleven months old. I cried continuously, baffled as to why this is happening to me? I tried to do everything right, yet everything went wrong. I was stressed, depressed and I felt like giving up. I thought *this life is too hard for me*. At this point, I didn't feel like I had much to live for. My second ex-husband had quickly moved on with his new family. He had a daughter with someone else, then, later on, had a son with her. After I was told we couldn't afford any more children. So when I gave birth to my son after being told I could no longer have children because of the abortion that tried to take me out during my first marriage. I told the doctors to tie my tubes. Make sure no more children come down that birth canal. I was happy yet afraid carrying my Demetrius. The pregnancy was quick but great! However, after experiencing all the disrespect, rejection and abandonment from husband number two, it left me feeling like no man is worth me ever getting pregnant for again. Just shut the factory all the way down. I remember feeling worthless and abandoned. I made up in my mind that I had had enough.

It was a nice, sunny Sunday morning, April 29, 2005, to be exact, I got up very weak and depressed. I asked myself what am I going to do? I have failed in life again, this time it's worse, it's not just me I have failed but a one-year-old as well. I not only have failed as a person but as a mother as well. Suicidal thoughts took place in my mind. I packed my son's diaper bag and placed my ID, bank cards, and all of his personal documents. I was planning to take him to mom's house, leave him, and return home to take as many pills as I could until I passed out, and hopefully died. I felt all of the dreams I had of dancing and helping others were all over, now. The dreams have ended, my life is a nightmare.

Then my one-year-old, Demetrius, came running around the corner at full speed as usual smiling and jumping up and down. I looked at him and cried harder, asking God why didn't He allow this kid to be born to much better parents? I turned the TV on, and a church program was playing. My son stopped and looked then started yelling, "CHURCH! CHURCH! CHURCH!"

I remember my son's father's cousin had previously been inviting me to her church. I remember constantly refusing her invite because I thought that nothing and no one could possibly understand what I am going through, let alone help. Not knowing then what I know now, that Philippians 4:7 says, "And the peace of God, which passeth all understanding shall keep your hearts, and minds through Christ Jesus.

After seeing what I thought was an unction from God to give him a try, I prepared for us to attend church. All I was thinking was that I have tried everything else - drinking, partying - and nothing has worked. I guess I will visit this church and see what happens. Why is it that we try everything and go to everyone before we try or go to God? Don't we know that God is all we need? My son and I were dressed and ready to go. The more I prepared to go the better I felt.

We made it!!! I was very nervous walking up the stairs of the church, but I kept going. Finally, I walked through the door, people were talking and laughing, it appeared they were having a good time. I thought what type of church is this, where people are happy? I had forgotten happiness still existed with all I have went through. Then people I did not know started walking towards my son and me, hugging and welcoming us.

I listened to the pastor, and his message was wonderful and clear. Instantly I felt human again, alive and hopeful. The pastor asked for all visitors to stand. I stood with nothing else to lose. I introduced my son and me and then asked for prayer for my family. I had surrendered, I was exhausted. Exhausted to the point where I didn't care who was looking, I broke down crying releasing my burden I was carrying. The people of God showed me love and embraced me – it was a good feeling that day.

God began to do a new work in me. I Corinthians 5:17 was real for me, I became a new creature. Several months passed and my son's father saw the change in me and started going to church with us. Because I wanted my family and I didn't want my son growing up without his father, like I did, I agreed to family counseling sessions. It may have seemed a little odd to some, but the counseling helped and eventually our family was together again.

NIETA S. DORTCH

Stronghold: Depression definition: from the American Psychiatric Association: Major depression disorder that negatively affects how you feel, the way you think, and how you act.

Scripture: Psalm 42:5 Message Bible- Why are you down in the dumps dear soul? Why are you crying the blues? Fix my eyes on God soon I'll be praising again. He puts a smile on my face, He's my God.

Prayer: God of God, Kings of Kings, I humbly come to you asking you to heal the minds and hearts of your people, especially those who have read this chapter. For we know that EVERYTHING start in our minds,

Wonderful people of God, please do this for me, lay your hands on your head and continue this prayer with me.

God heal my mind, set me free from the spirit of depression. Let this mind be in me that was also in Christ Jesus. Let me begin to think on those things that are lovely, pure, and of good report. The word of God says nothing is too impossible for me, God. Spirit of depression I command you to get out of the minds of Gods people, NOW, in the mighty name of Jesus. Flee now! God your word says resist the devil, and he shall flee. As I begin/continue to resist the spirit of depression by thinking on your promises, I shall be delivered. Amen!

The Vision Is Birthed - Habakkuk 2:3

Chapter Three

Here it is, October 2005, and we had our first church meeting. At the time I didn't know that the church was in the beginning stages of its ministry. It was exciting to be a part of this meeting because we were able to talk about any ideas we might have had regarding forming auxiliary ministries in the church. It's not going to take a rocket scientist to figure out what I presented. You already know praise dancing. As I was telling my ideas, the more I talked, the more joy I felt in my heart.

The next day I received a call from the church administrator explaining that the pastor loved my idea and that he would like a detailed proposal ASAP. I prayed and prepared, then submitted the proposal that week. Two weeks later I received a letter in the mail saying that my idea was approved and that took me to another level spiritually. The letter also requested that I form and prepare a team to go forth at our New Year's Eve service - less than two months away. Then I stopped and, "said wait a minute," I never praise danced before and truthfully never saw it done.

I called my big sister, Michelle and asked her if she knew someone who could help me? Or have any tapes? She gave me a VHS tape of an old praise dance routine from a church. As I watched, I was like, *Oh, OK*, but something inside of me said that is nice but that's not what God is calling me to do, He had a different dance. He had a different dance He wanted me to present to the world. I began to hit my knees constantly in prayer seeking guidance from God. Finally, He gave me a vision, and I gathered six young ladies in the church, and we went to work. The Bible says, "Ask so you shall receive so your joy can be full."

The New Year's Eve service was awesome. God showed up and out. The pastor was pleased, and so was the congregation. The dance ministry was going well. As a team, we were having a ball. However, anything done to glorify God enrages the enemy. Right in the church, in the camp, the devil pulled it. Saints, if all we have is religion and not a relationship with God, we are very much opened to being used by the devil. So of course opposition came. Certain members felt since their daughter - thirteen year old - had been a member longer she should have been the leader. Then another member felt since her sister used to dance and choreograph back in the day, that had I not put the proposal in her sister would be in charge. Wow, what happened? Doesn't the Bible, the Holy Bible, speak on covertness? And besides, the ministry was still fairly new. They really didn't have a much longer membership than I had.

    In the meantime, the company I had worked for was a family owned business and all of a sudden the owner decided to sell. So now, no job for me after I put in almost 10 years into this company and I was having this issue with the dance ministry at the church. Things only escalated from there, without a job I wasn't able to give in tithes and offering the way I use to – this put a strain on my relationship with the church even further. You would have thought they would have empathetic to my situation, but they weren't. It was a snowball of events, my marriage started to go through again, and I found myself back on my knees asking God to help me.

On Father's Day 2007, I was approached after service by the First Lady and the sisters, telling me the pastor wasn't feeling my work any longer. Yes, those were her exact words. She said he felt that I should hand the dance ministry over to the sister. Out of obedience because it was his church and the dance ministry belong to that church, I obeyed. Saints, we must be careful to not get weary in well doing for in due season we will reap if we faint not (Galatians 6:9). Saints, I must admit I fainted. Out of disbelief, I struggled spiritually. I struggled with how God-fearing people could behave like that. However, deep in my spirit I always believed that was not the end. I know that what God put in me wasn't over.

Stronghold: Covetousness definition: English dictionary: Wanting to have something too much, especially something that belong to someone else.

Scripture: Jeremiah 6:13 From the least of them even unto the greatest of them everyone is given to covetousness, and from the prophet, even unto the priest every one dealeth falsely.

Prayer: Father God, only you know what lies deep in our hearts. God, I ask you to search our hearts, and if you find ANYTHING unclean or any spirit of jealousy or anything not like you, I ask you to forgive me and uproot that spirit from me, now, in the mighty name of Jesus. Let me come to you seeking what you have for me, not looking at what you've given others. God when we don't know who we are or our purpose, it will allow us to look and want what others have. God, please free our minds, hearts to see what you, Daddy God, have for me to see, and do what you want us to do so we can have what you want us to have. Free our hearts and minds, so we receive it all in Jesus mighty name, Amen.

When Man says, No…. But God says, Yes!! – Luke 1:37

Chapter Four

I was always told that people are in your life for a reason, season, or lifetime. It's up to you to seek God for guidance as to where they belong. The pain I felt behind all that happened was horrific and humiliating. Not only was I removed as the praise dance leader, I was told I couldn't even dance because of decisions my then husband at that time had made. Returning to one of his baby mommas again. However, I kept going to church, I kept worshipping God, I kept giving my time, talent, and treasure. One day I received an email with an encouraging word, it read: "knocking me down was easy, but keeping me down would take an army." I am a child of God, and one thing I do know is God will never leave or forsake me. I kept studying my word, and I continued to tell others about our great God. Saints, when persecution comes our way, and trust me it will, we must go harder for God. Draw closer to God. If you get knocked down so low just reach for the hem of His garment. Believe me, when I say this, God is always right there, He never moves away from us. We may move (run) away from Him, but He's always right there, willing and able to see us through.

I felt so low, so unworthy because of what happened to me. Some of the church members didn't agree and relocated to another church. I stayed because I wasn't led by God at that time to move on. My husband at that time was very upset and felt that his decisions shouldn't change my place in the church and that he couldn't continue going to such a place. Again, our marriage went through. My ex-husband relocated to New Life Covenant Oakwood where Pastor John F. Hannah delivers powerful, life-changing sermons week after week. Again, I stayed alone, hurting, asking God why? And asking Him to see me through.

I was offered a job at a Catholic school in 2008 to teach praise dancing there. I spoke to the First Lady of my church about it, and after much consideration, I accepted the position. The process begun and I thanked God for another chance. Remember Saints, what the devil meant for evil,

God will use it for your good. Praise God, I was asked to resume dancing at the church. Of course, I prayed about it and accepted, because my dance belonged to God not man - plus I knew God wasn't through with me there, yet. I am a worshipper. I cannot sit still and worship God. The Bible says, "We must worship God in spirit and in truth."

At the school, I was free to pray with the children and explain the purpose of dancing for God. The school dance ministry grew, and I then planed an end of the year recital to draw the families in to see God's work. Also to see what warfare these children were facing at home. My classes were more than just teaching dance. They were designed to lead the youth to God. At times, these children get built up spiritually then return home trying to live the Bible, but it's often refused and shot down in their homes. Once I met the parent(s) or caregivers, that then gave me a better direction on how to layout and cover those children and their homes in prayer.

There may be times when it appears as if we are losing. At times we might have to look as if we are losing in order to win. It doesn't matter if someone does not agree with the call on your life or even speak that it won't happen. It's not up to them to see or understand the vision/calling God birthed you for. Rather they agree or not you stay true to it even when you don't understand. As long as it's from God, man may say no, but God will say yes. God will say, "Child of mine, keep praying keep pressing. It might not make sense now, but you'll soon see." And God will get the glory.

When Others Forsake You - Deuteronomy 31:6
Chapter Five

Remember in the previous chapter I stated that people are in your life for a reason, season, and lifetime? Being connected to God will allow you to be properly place people in the correct category. Our flesh will ALWAYS telling us to do things, Saints, but we must be Spirit-led and not flesh-led. Saints, the spirit is always willing, but the flesh is weak. I shamed the enemy. I returned to the dance team at church, and I danced like never before. I was obedient to the leader, one of the sisters, and I had a pure heart. The Bible says, "Be faithful over a few things and God would make you ruler over many."

By this time the enemy was confused. He probably was thinking, how is she still worshipping and praising God when this should have taken her down? Saints, we must remember God will never put more on us than we can bear. Everything He allows is being used to mold us to be all He created us to be. Opposition hits again. I was told the real reason I was removed as the dance leader. I was truly blown away. The reason I was previously given wasn't the truth at all. I remember finding out that because my tithes had decreased and my son's father and I were no longer together (he'd went back to his other children's mother) that I was no longer as valuable as once before. I had no income, and I was back taking care of my son alone. In this ministry, to be in leadership, you basically had to be in a position to give more than the lay members. The small income source that I had coming in wasn't enough in their minds.

    I fought that thing naturally until literally, I became sick in my body. Then I heard a voice say, *this battle is not yours but the Lords.* I was ill in my body for three months. The doctors were confused as to why things were not working. I then begin to cry out to God, and I did a spiritual check on myself. I asked God what was I doing wrong? Am I outside your will? I felt so disconnected. During your spiritual walk, you will learn those feelings that are alerting you that you are doing something wrong, or heading in the wrong direction, just totally outside of His will.

During that time, in 2010, God was birthing something great in me. Out of respect, I presented my business plan to my pastor because I looked up to him and I wanted his input. Besides everything else that had gone on, he was a great businessman. He said it was awesome and that I should go for it. He asked all the members to pray that all goes well with my business. Shortly after I was intrigued that he asked me to meet at a coffee shop to talk about my business plan and to bring it with me. I met but without my business plan. Saints, when you are connected, God will never allow you to just walk into a set up without already speaking to you on how to handle it. At the meeting, he asked me to hand over my business plan, that it was great, and that he could use it to grow and benefit the body of Christ. However, he felt that one of the sisters should present it to the world since she had a college degree and was stable in her marriage. But his last reasoning blow me away, he said he felt that she was more qualified to carry it out.

"God birthed this through me, and you want me to just hand it over?" I asked him. Forming a dance ministry in his church and being obedient to hand it over is one thing. But God birthing something in me and me just hand it over is another thing. Because I knew God birthed it in me, I knew not to hand it over. Looking back on this experience it reminds me of one of Pastor Hannah's teaching, he teaches us to fight for our kingdom.

I remember crying out to God again because I started several other ministries in that church but they were quickly handed over to other people, so I thought maybe my job is to seek God, allow Him to channel it through me then pass it along. If that is the case, God show me so that I can stay in your will. God quickly reminded me that I don't call those that are qualified, I qualify those I call.

I was then led to study on Moses, Paul, and Abraham. The pastor then changed his request telling those members who had stepped up to help me that if anyone were found helping me, they would be asked to leave his church. And of course, we were all babes in Christ when we joined his church and felt obligated to do what he said. I did the same thing to others who left before me. I pulled back and didn't reach out to those hurting people because he said not to. He had us fearful that if he let us go from his church that all hell would break through in our lives. We believed him because a previous family left because of his ways and months later their son was killed. He explained to us that the family suffered because they left his church. I didn't recognize the spirit of control that the pastor had over his congregation.

The members resigned from helping me. I cried to God wondering how I was supposed to carry out his plan alone? I was trying to be obedient, I couldn't understand why things were going wrong? One of Pastor Hannah's DVDs that my ex-husband had purchased one time during a visit and gave it to me kept flashing in my face. Even though our journey was what it was, with my ex-husband and I, God still used him to get me to my safe place. My son's father was ordained to be a part of my journey but not to go all the way. I did not know to seek God when we met to determine if he was a season, reason, or a lifetime person. He looked good, and we hooked up. He was a great provider, and he gave me total freedom. So I thought he was the one, so I married that man.

As I was watching the DVD, I found myself face down in my living room crying out to God. I then received my next set of instructions. I then fell again on my knees repenting to God for my disobedience. Yes, as you see, I have a degree in kneeology. It's all I know to do. I received the instructions before, but my loyalty got in the way. When I am loyal, I am loyal 100% - it seemed as if everyone has forsaken me but my God was still right there.

I'VE BEEN RELEASED

Encourage Yourself – 1st Samuel 30:60

Chapter Six

I was broken because man had turned their backs on me. Saints, when God is preparing us for our next level in Him, He will allow people to do, and not do, certain things. It may seem like a wilderness period. There are times God wants us all to Himself. In that place, He will love on you, direct you, protect you, and most of all, bless you. In that place we are uncomfortable. Why? Because we are out of our comfort zone, a place the flesh doesn't like to be.

We love to say, God, I am waiting on you, but the reality is God is waiting on us. There comes a time when it seems that everything around us is going wrong, but somehow you are being led to keep going in spite of.

At times we, our flesh, look for that pat on the back, someone to say "job well done." But in that season it won't come because God has cuffed you and directed you to follow, listen, and to obey only Him. Which builds that intimacy and personal relationship with God. He never intended for you always only to be fed by your Shepard but to learn to feed yourself until Sunday comes. That way your spiritual muscles are strengthened, and soon or later you can assist your Shepard with the vision of the house you are connected to. Serving the servants forever cannot be the plan. It's souls to be won - well, that's another book.

During that time you must learn to encourage yourself. After all, who's approval are you seeking? God's approval? Or man's approval? Saints, I've tried both, and take it from me, God's approval is what we must seek and it's more rewarding.

The power of life and death is in our tongue. So be very careful what you release into the atmosphere. The Bible says, speak those things that's not as though they were. When you need encouragement, and trust me you will, began to pray more, study more, and worship more. In that place, you will have more than what's needed.

As time progressed in my story, 2011 came upon me quickly, and I am now at New Life, and was amazing!!! The level of worship and anointing in the building is mind-blowing. Instantly my spirit man connected. I felt like a kidnapped child that was finally brought back home. I was amazed at all the people that gathered in one place, at the same time, to worship God and to hear a word from Him.

At this time I understood my next level of instructions, what I heard in the spirit had manifested in the natural. Obedience will lead you into God's will for your life, and it will be remarkable! It had brought me to a place that God allowed for healing in my spiritual, physical, mental, life to occur and I gained financial growth. The praise team was singing, "No more shackles, no more chains, no more bondage, I am free, yeah!!!" As I think on the scene, I remember tears flowing down my face. I said to myself, I am at New Life and it is truly time for my new life.

As I looked around at what was going on, I spotted a cage on the stage. Because I was familiar with Pastor Hannah's teaching style, I was excited to see how God had led him to deliver today's message. But never in a million years was I prepared for what I experienced. A young lady entered the stage dressed in dark clothing and went in the cage and covered herself up. Pastor Hannah began to speak on how we allow people to back us in. Again, the tears flowed faster this time and harder. Talk about being at the right place at the right time – I needed this message.

I began to say within myself, "I'm free, I can make it. Oh, God. I thank you, thank you, Jesus!!! I am going to be all God created me to be." I was determined that no weapon that formed against me was going to be able to prosper (Isaiah 54:17). Nothing was too hard for God.

When To Let Go! – Matthew 10:14

Chapter Seven

God is awesome!!!! I have a new life. I am dreaming again and setting goals. I am ready to walk into my destiny. But at times I have flashbacks of the times I trusted people, those in positions and they hurt and deceived me, lied on me, mistreated me, and abandon me. But Saints that's why the word of God is so powerful, sharper than any two-edged sword. The Bible says, "when people mistreat you, speak evil against you falsely, greater is your reward in heaven." I LOVE THE BIBLE!!!!! With that being said, I ain't got no worries!

The enemy is so cunning. He likes to bring up your past and all the things that's associated with it. The pain, shame, guilt only to keep you down in bondage. Hoping you will go or return to depression, and jump back slide with him. But you must speak to that voice and remind it that I am more than a conquer!!!! When the enemy brings your past up, it's like having a wound that has finally formed a scab, and he keeps snatching the scab off so that the wound would never heal. That way the wound would hurt, bleed, and the healing process will have to start all over, causing distractions and time delays in your mission and purpose. Remember Saints, delayed doesn't mean denied. What God started He will finish.

Saints, God has instructions - His Word - for us to follow. In order to live out His will for our lives, we must have obedience! Here is that powerful word that will lead us to our destinies. However, the opposite is true as well, disobedience will definitely lead us places God never intended for us to go -free will. Just like a doctor gives instructions and medicine to help, whatever we are facing we can be healed or helped with our problems or illnesses. If we follow God's instructions with obedience, we can heal as if it was never there. Well God also has instructions right in His word, the Bible, which teaches us how to heal spiritually by repenting and casting our cares to Him. The scars can heal and never return through God's healing power. Heaven offers protection so that the enemy can never use that scar to defeat you any longer.

The Bible says, resist (fight) the devil and he shall flee. The only way to resist him is with God's word. You cannot fight this alone. You are no match for the enemy. The Bible says in Ephesians 6:12-13, "for we wrestle not against flesh and blood, but against the rulers of the darkness of this world, against spiritual wickedness in high places. Wherefore take unto you the whole armor of God that ye may be able to withstand in the evil day, and having done all, to stand".

When you build yourself upon God's word, you, too, can fight and command Satan, in the mighty name of Jesus to flee from you. When he sees that he can longer trick you or use that tactic any longer, he will then instruct his band of demons to leave you alone.

The next time I saw any of those people, I greeted them with a genuine smile, and I knew in my heart that my God had fought all of my battles for me. I can't afford to waste His precious time, fighting fights when there are wars out here to be won for the kingdom of God. Then you are able to "let go and let God."

After all, the people that hurt you never expect them to apologize to you. If you never forgive them, that gives them power over your life. Now ask yourself, are they worth it? Are they that important to have your life on pause? If your life is still consumed by this, then you are no benefit to the kingdom of God. Now you are giving man more power over your life than God.

Saints, I know that is not what you want. Matthew 10:14 says, "And whosoever will not receive you, nor hear your words, when ye depart out of that house or city, shake the dust off your feet." These are the words of our Lord and Saviour Jesus Christ. So free yourself and let go.

Pastor Hannah taught a sermon titled: "What Does It Matter?" When unimportant flashbacks would occur, I would yell out, WHAT DOES IT MATTER!!! And immediately it would be released from my spirit.

I'VE BEEN RELEASED

Fight For God's Truth – Jude 1:17-23

Chapter Eight

When God says so, remember it is so! Our thoughts are not His thoughts, our ways are not His ways, as far as the heaven is above the earth that's how far His thoughts are above ours. When God deposits His kingdom into you, it's up to you to fight for your kingdom. Saints, it's like giving birth to a child. Once the seed is planted and starts to grow, you begin to nourish it to full term. The excitement of it being born is unexplainable. Once the baby arrives, another level of nourishment and work begins. As parents, we do all we can to provide, protect, and comfort our child(ren). Come on Saints, that's what you must do with your kingdom. Protect it by any means necessary.

The enemy only comes to steal, kill, and destroy. Be careful who you pick up on this journey. The enemy is seeking whom he may devour. Having a strong spirit of discernment is crucial in this stage. My pastor teaches us that people can be attracted to your anointing, they don't want you, they are after your anointing. WOW, right? Trust and believe that spirit won't stop until it defeats you, or you defeat it.

How do we fight for God's truth? I am glad you asked. The only way to fight for God's truth is with God's word. The word of God works every time. Saints, the word is powerful, it's true, it's life-changing and most important - IT WILL NOT COME BACK VOID!

In our church, our pastor pushes us to be all God called and created us to be. He is never intimidated. He always motivates us. At times he gets so mad in the spirit, when he sees us looking defeated, that he will begin to cry out in the spirit for a word to help us. And God being God does delivers a word through our pastor to help us get over that hump.

Saints, we often get weary when the dots aren't connecting. When we don't see a way out. Then fear sets in, that's why I love the Bible. The Word declares, "He didn't give us a spirit of fear, but of power, love and a sound mind" (2 Timothy 1:7).

Saints, for every mountain, problem, and situation, or storm there is a word from God to guide you through it. The Bible says, "Study to show thyself approved." In the natural realm (real life), when we study for a test/exam in school, work, or etc. On test day we are confident that we will pass. That is how we must be in the spirit realm. A word from a wise man, "No punks allowed" when it comes to fighting in the kingdom.

God is looking for a generation who will fight for Him, not against Him. Who will live a sacrificial life unto Him? Jesus said to be a disciple for Him it's three things we must do. 1. Deny ourselves. 2. Pick up our cross. 3. Follow Him. It's amazing how He would first start off with the denying ourselves part. Because Jesus knew no good thing dwells in our flesh, the flesh wants what it wants when it wants it. The flesh doesn't like to hear no. God would never ask us to do His job. So why are you trying to do his? He is God!!! He is strong, mighty, and excellent in all His ways. Saints, remember the race isn't given to the swift, nor to the strong, but to he who endures to the end. FIGHT! FIGHT!! FIGHT!!!

I'VE BEEN RELEASED

Fulfilling Your God-Given Purpose – Romans 8:28

Chapter Nine

Wow!!!! Here I am in 2012. I am now the founder and director of Release Dance Productions (RDP). As of 2015, it was renamed Release Dance Ministry (RDM). Our motto is "Not Just Teaching Dance, But Birthing Worshippers." It is a biblical based dance ministry, where the word of God is our foundation. Everything we do is done to glorify our God. Here at Release we teach and learn to live God's word out in our lives daily. Our worshippers (dancers) ages have ranged from five years old throughout adulthood. Where our youngest member at a point was four years old, and she was very talented, and our oldest member has been fifty-five years old. Release had touched the lives of over eighty children, not including the word of God reaching their homes and touching family members as well.

Only when we are obedient and say yes to God's will for our lives can we be a benefit to God's kingdom. Doing it God's way and not our way can, and will, lead to some amazing breakthroughs. When our lives are God-centered and not self- centered He can use us in mighty ways. Things will spring out of us we never knew were there.

We were all put here for a purpose or a special task, but until we connect to God, we will never recognize it. God must know that He can trust us to fulfill such a task. We are all pieces of this great, big old puzzle, and every piece is needed to complete God's will or need for this world. What piece are you holding? Are you connected and dedicated to God? If so let's go!!!! If not, what are you waiting on? Who hindered you? God is able to do exceedingly and abundantly above all we could ever ask or think (Ephesians 3:20).

Remember Saints, God did not give us a spirit of fear but of power, love, and a sound mind. Launch out!!!! If it weren't for you, He would have never placed it in you. Who is holding you back? Who has spoken negative words over your life? Remember in a previous chapter I mentioned, *what does it matter*? Take the power back!!!

Remember our God is bigger and stronger. He is higher than any other. You must see the vision. It's not for others to point it out to you. It's your God-given purpose, it's in you. I don't care what you've been through, it doesn't cancel God's plan for your life. Here is proof. Genesis 50:20 says, "What the devil meant for evil, God will turn it around and use it for your good."

When God gave Joseph a dream, He never reminded Joseph of that dream again. We all know the story of Joseph, aka The Dreamer. Joseph told his dream to his father and brothers, which only led him into being sold into slavery, lied on by the king's wifey, imprisoned and forgotten. But after all, was said and done, Joseph still sat on that throne, and had to deliver some of the same ones that rose up against him – he was walking in his God-given purpose. Funny how God will have the very people who rose up against you who tried to kill your purpose. Need the very thing God put in you. Or use the person who betrayed you to bless you - that's another book there.

I will never tell you that fulfilling your God-given purpose will be easy. But I can tell you, it's worth it. God has a plan and purpose for you, too. Do you know what it is? For those who know what I am talking about was it easy? No, but we kept pressing and so can you. If you haven't started, get started. Someone's breakthrough is tied to it. God birthed this book through me for you. Someone is crying to God for help. Is their help locked up in you? Someone wants to be released. There is a ministry inside us all. What are you waiting for? Who are you waiting on? It's what God created you to do. You belong to God and so does EVERYTHING that's connected to you, which included your purpose. Remember your life is not your own. Surrender today and fulfill your God-given purpose.

I've Been Released - Romans 8:36

Chapter Ten

In early 2013 my pastor began telling us to prepare for the supernatural. He shared his personal testimony about his preparation which led to where he is now. He is extremely funny, but he keeps it real. Before this message, I had already had a vision of myself on TV doing some type of an interview, telling the world how awesome our God is. I thought it was about Release Dance, but now I am fully assured that it is not. My Pastor gave us different examples about him going to the dentist and etc., basically a quick run through of the things he was instructed to do as he prepared for greater. For years I struggled out of fear to have this facial surgery that was not life or death, but according to the doctors it was considered, by medical standards to have a facial disfigurement. For years I was very self-conscience about it. I would not ever wear my hair up because I needed to cover both sides of my face around the jaw area. I allowed that sermon to get in my spirit and at last, I contacted the doctor.

Around early Fall 2013, I began to feel constant pain in my legs. Gradually the pain increased, and I begin to lose weight, to the sum of over fifty pounds. The doctors ran all type of test, but no answers. All test were coming back very grim, basically saying that my body was shutting down. They determined that what was already in my body was not the problem. By January 2014 I could hardly walk, at times I would fall and did not have enough strength to pick myself back up. Wow, right! Eight months later I felt and looked horrible, my body was fighting hard to stay alive. Again, more tests were taken, but nothing was found. I could not eat or sleep, most of all by now I couldn't walk without assistance. We are taught that the very thing you loved, and are called to do the enemy would come after that thing, and for me, it was dancing for God.

One day out of the blue my son, who was ten years old at the time, came and asked, "Mommy, how are you feeling?" I remember telling him that I wasn't doing good.

This powerful little boy then said, "God said you are on a journey." I was shocked by what he said. He was too young to be spiritual, so I thought, so I was confused to what made him say such a thing.

"A journey?" I asked.

"Yes, a two-year journey." He responded. I immediately wanted to scream because there was no way I could see myself suffering like this for two years. He continued, "But God said you are going to be alright, mommy when this is over." Then he kissed me on my head said, "I gotta go. Daddy made me some chicken nuggets." He just dropped that bomb and left. Wow, out of the mouth of babes.

In June 2014 my family decided that I should try another hospital, I did and was admitted after my second trip to the ER. There my family and twenty-plus friends were watching me as what appeared to be my last days. I cried out to God because I knew as a woman of God I was not exempt from life tragedies, but this right here just did not add up. I asked why is this happening to me? What did I do wrong? What did I do to deserve this? Then clearly I heard a voice say, "preparation." I am thinking for what? My funeral? Then I hear, "Preparation for your next level. When I bring you out of this, all will see the hand of God is all on you."

In a Thursday night Bible study my pastor mentioned during his message that things will get worse before they would get better. That again was one of the things my spirit snatched up. I began praying and rebuking because everything in me said that applies to you and your health. I tried that spirit to see if it was of God, and Saints, it was. Well, the Bible does say, *should we accept the good only from God and not the bad?* Let me clear something up, though. God does not put bad things on anyone, but he will allow them to get you where he wants you. Or maybe even to get your attention.

Now I am admitted in the hospital, and after a few days, I am diagnosed with lupus. What??? Me? As if I already did not have enough going on in my body.

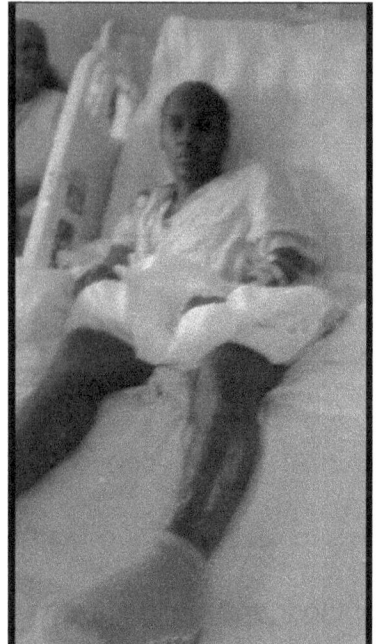 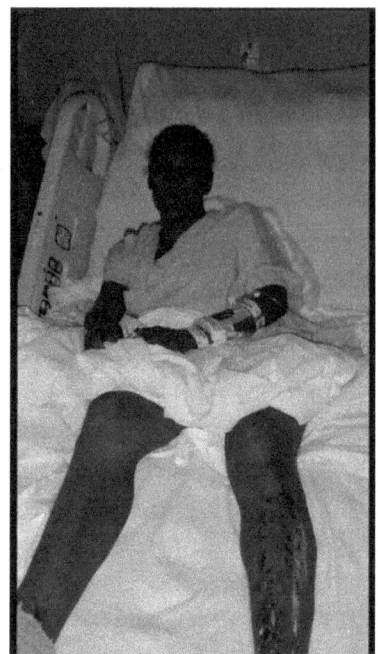

Hospital pictures during lupus attack.

Saints, no matter what we go through, remember God will not put more on us than we can bear – I can't say that enough. I had to undergo a bone marrow, several biopsies, blood transfusions - you name it, I received it. The doctors were for sure that the lupus had damaged some, if not all of my organs, but God!!! The weapons will form, but they would not prosper. Hallelujah!!! My hair had stopped growing and thinned out tremendously on my head, blood had stopped flowing. I said God you are allowing this for a reason. It doesn't look or feel good, but not my will, Lord, but your will be done.

On July 4th I wanted to give up. This was too much for one person. I thought about how I had laid in that hospital bed for nineteen days now, and all odds were against me. I started to submit to the sickness and have a defeated mindset. A lot crossed my heart, mind, and spirit. Should I let go? I am tired of fighting battles only to lose every battle. People I thought that should have been there wasn't, and those I did not think would was. But something in the inside of me wouldn't allow my thoughts to go too far. As I sat in a dark room alone, no TV or lights, because my family and twenty-plus friends had been at that hospital night and day, every day, I told everyone to stay home and enjoy the holiday with their families. I told them I would be alright as I needed time alone, but quickly I found out I wasn't. That was the darkest day of that journey. I could have made one call, and they would have all rushed to the hospital to see me.

But I love to see everyone else happy and enjoying life even when I cannot.

Then I felt a strong presence in the room with me. I asked, "Who is there?" No one answered. The presence got stronger, I became afraid. I ask again, "Who is there?" At this time I was thinking maybe it is the death angel coming to get me. Do not ask me where that came from, I do not know, but quickly I changed my mind about letting go. I became scared I wasn't ready to see what the afterlife looked like. I was determined not to die alone in that hospital. I realized that I could die and had yet to experience life to its fullest really. It was a lot of places and things I have never seen or done.

Suddenly I felt a finger touch my left big toe and the feeling rose up to my knee on the same leg. This was the same leg that the doctors told my mom that the nerve damage was so severe that there was a twenty-five percent chance I would ever walk again. But my mom being the woman of God, immediately laughed in those doctors faces when they said it. I remember her asking me sternly, "Whose report are you going to believe?" Again, I could not see anyone in that dark room, and I could not get up and walk anywhere. I had knocked the call nurse pad on the floor so I could not press for help. Then a spirit of peace came over me, and I guess I went to sleep because I woke up and it was light outside. The last time I checked the time, before that encounter, it was 9:02pm. Wow, peace and sweet rest in the midst of the storm. Nobody but God. That morning I felt like praying for strength and endurance. The Bible does say, "ask, and you shall receive, seek, and ye shall find, knock and it shall be opened unto you." One thing I am confident in is that the word of God is true. And I have learned it will not come back void.

I began to get stronger, then my healing process began. The doctors went from looking helpless to looking amazed. I began to witness to the doctors, nurses, cleaning crew and anyone who entered my room or handled me in any shape or form. Their perception was still the same, this girl has one foot in the grave and the other on earth still talking about God. I told the devil I am in a win/win state. If I leave here, I am going to heaven, if I stay, then my job is not finished, and my work will be greater. I know from then to now the enemy was wishing he had his way.

I began to see myself walking and living and enjoying life. I told myself I had to get out that bed and walk, and get those pampers off. I was a child of God. His word says, "He healeth all manner of sickness and disease, and by His stripes I am healed." During that time I spoke the word over my life vehemently. I kept saying to myself, "speak those things that's not as though they were." Then God went to work on me like never before. We must remember when we ask God for something it's up to Him how and when He wants it done. God always blows my mind.

The love and support I received was amazing, it was part of what helped carry me through. God even restored some relationships I thought were done and finished. Now the doctor finally say that it's time for me to be discharged from the hospital. Yes, you heard right, I am about to leave the hospital to heal, and not in a body bag.

But the discharge was bittersweet, I was told that I would have to go to rehab to learn to care for yourself again. I didn't want to receive that, I was ready to go home, not be in another hospital-like facility. The doctors explain that I am not strong enough to climb the three flights of stairs and to be able to return to my doctor appointments on a weekly basis without assistance. Knowing then what I know now God knew exactly what He was doing, home was the last place I needed to be at that time.

But I can't help thinking, rehab? The way I felt at the time, I did not need a rehab center. I felt strong. It was probably due to the excitement of being discharged. I thought I was going to be alright. The outside just had not caught up with the inside, yet. I was feeling stronger and healed, and I chose to believe that nothing was too impossible for God. I began to cry out and pray to God about the rehab center. Closer to my discharge date the head physical and occupational therapist paid me a visit. He came to re-evaluate me because of the report of the first physical therapist. What was in the report was unbelievable to them, so they decided he needed to see for himself. I'm telling you all, where I was on this day from the previous week was like night and day.

During the evaluation, one of the nurses said I was very strong and determined, and seemed like a woman that liked a challenge. I explained to them that I believed challenges push you and make you stronger and better. They bring out things in you that you never knew existed. He smiles as I returned to my bed. Boy, was I struggling but I made it. He placed his hand on my shoulder and said, keep believing and pushing, and you will be alright. Look at God performing a miracle right in front of those doctors. In their report, they stated that I was too strong to go to any facility and that no facility would accept me.

Then a word was sent to me that I would have a speedy recovery and I did. Thank you, Jesus!!!!! What the devil meant for evil God was turning it around for my good. God allowed this for a reason, reasons I might find out here on earth or in heaven or never. I am no longer trying to figure it out. I am just enjoying life and trying to be obedient to His will for my life - easier said than done at times. However, all I know is my life is in His hands, and He is in control. God will get the glory out of my life, plus He knows He can trust me with this testimony. The world would soon see and hear and believe that God is still a healer, He still does miracles today.

Today I am walking, running, and I have gained thirty pounds of my weight back. And after much healing and consideration, I have decided I am good where I am. I am enjoying life more and more. My son and I have traveled places I never thought before to travel, and the best is yet to come. God totally comforted my son during that time and placed some great families around him to love on him and keep him busy. A special thanks to the Pipkin and Murray Families. My faith is so much stronger now. I went through for nine months. Wow, the same length of time to carry a child. See a seed of ministry was placed in the inside of me and now it's the birthing time. A ministry is coming forth out of me. The fire, or test, will never feel good, but the ministry that God births in you will be priceless. Look at the price Jesus paid for us all. Jesus, our Lord, and Saviour said we will do greater works. What did the older people use to say? What doesn't kill you will make you stronger. I am still here, and my faith is stronger than it has ever been. I have been healed by the blood of the Lamb. God has snatched me from the hand of the enemy. Thank you, Jesus, I Have Been Released.

Certain relationships did not make this journey with me. Which turned into another journey after I was discharged. It was a battle that God prepared me for spiritually so but knocked me off my feet naturally so. The day I was discharged I found out just how much strength I had. I was so excited I shocked myself with the things I did as I prepared to leave. All I was thinking was finally I am out of here, and I want to leave before something happens, and they say one more day. I called my husband at that time praying he would answer because I needed a ride.

Here's a little recap – because I know I've talked so much you forgot my husband was in the picture - I barely heard from him since going into the hospital. The time frame was more like from June 18 of that year to July 20 of that same year. He brought my son to see me once and complained about parking the entire twenty-five minutes they were there.

The day I was leaving the hospital as I was calling him he answers the phone, I tell him I need a ride to my mom's house because the doctors thought that location was best because she lived on the first floor and I could easily return to my appointments. He explains that he was not able to pick me up from the hospital. I tell him, "OK" and hang up. I turn over and cried for a moment, then got myself together and said let me find a ride. I know my family will have a lot of questions, now. I was slightly ashamed to face them because I had made excuses for him this entire time. Little did I know they already figured it out but did not involve me because they wanted me to get better.

I made it to my mom's house and stayed there for another eleven days. My mom was exhausted from sleepless nights before and after I was admitted in the hospital and now I am back at her home. My niece, Torria would come over during the day to help take care of me. My other niece, Wendy (Marlene) brought the boys over, and they stayed some nights with me. My heart was full of joy.

I was beginning to feel sorry for my mom, though because she was doing a lot for me without a lot of help. I recall her telling me how one day she left the hospital and she was completely worn out and weary. She said as soon as she made it inside the house she fell to her knees crying. She recalls crying out to God asking Him to please not take his baby girl, not to let me die. She asked God if anyone had to die to let it be her, but please not to take her baby girl. A mother's love is unconditional. But God had another plan.

I got stronger and began to walk with a walker. My appetite came back full force – I contribute that to the steroids they had me on. Some of my weight returned little by little. I had doctor's appointments several times a week. My mom and I took a transportation service to and from my appointments. Again, where is my husband? Why isn't he here? I knew healing was my first priority so that I could return to my son and my business – I didn't have time to worry about what he was doing. I knew all I needed to know about my marriage at that time, so healing was step one.

I called him because I wanted to see my son. Every time I called, he made me feel like I was bothering him. I didn't care because I wanted to see my son, but I would get off the phone and cry. I would just say, "God, I want to see my son, please work it out." One day he finally decides to bring my son to me on his off day. I was so excited because I had missed my baby. I told my son to bring all the board games so we could have a blast. He arrives with the games, and I could not have been more excited. I could not go anywhere, but to my doctor's appointments, so I had to make the best out of the situation. My son was overwhelmed to see me. Even though I still didn't look like myself, he still hugged and loved me the same.

I'm back once again to my doctor, and I'm being examined for my progress. My doctor was happy to still see me smiling and my mom still by my side. However, my mom needed a break so we decided that I would now go a few blocks away to my niece's, Torria, house. There I got stronger and began to bathe myself again, and I gained control of my bladder, look at God. I could now walk up and down the stairs alone, albeit slowly, but at least I was doing it.

I'm finally doing much better to a point which all my doctors agree it would be a good idea to return home. August 6 I go home. My mom insisted on going with me. A transportation company takes us to my house, and my friends meet me to help bring my bags up and get me situated in the house. She had movies and food waiting for me to welcome me home. My son was so happy you would have thought it was Christmas morning. Again, where is my husband? I know right. He said he would play ball with his friends and then go straight to work. When he came home the next day he was full of anger. My thought, *is he mad that I didn't die*? Sound crazy, huh? Well, keep reading.

Here I am, alive and getting back to being healthy, but in my home, my son was the only one sharing in the joy with me. I prayed and fasted and anointed my home and all his belongings believing God could and would turn this around. Saints, remember God sees and knows all, and He will not bless no mess unless there are two repentant hearts. In this case, it was only one.

In October 2014 the enemy was fully exposed in my marriage. One of my spiritual advisors told me when I was leaving my mom's house that when I returned home to stay in prayer and don't question much. She prophesied that in thirty days God will expose everything I needed to know. I obeyed even though the first day I was home I had enough evidence to end it all. But I still believed God. That journey lasted until November, Thanksgiving Eve to be exact. He left a note stating he will be back in a couple of days. What??? Where do they do that at??? I still held on to my faith. On November 30th I received a powerful word at church, no one knew what was going on in my home, No family or friends. The sermon was entitled, "Let Lot Go," and I received a breakthrough. I cried for God to rescue my son and I because I refused to believe that God pulled me out that hospital to live like this. When I returned home from church told me we needed to talk. We had a long conversation, and then he departed from our home. Outside of my near-death experience, this would prove to be yet another Hard battle that God would deliver me out of.

We were left without heat and an income, now my marriage of sixteen years was over. I asked God to please show me what happened? I heard loud and clear during a service at church one Sunday that he had failed his assignment, but I held on. God revealed to me that the blessings he was going to pour on me that my ex-husband was not going to be able to receive. While I was lying in the hospital bed, my husband had fell for someone he met on a dating site - unbelievable. I believe it's still a purpose for my pain.

December 10th that year our divorce case was finished and settled. I was happy that it was over. My attorney was amazing. Even the judge told me to tell her job well done. See where God's will is and where He will take you everyone cannot go. Remember in chapter 5 I stated people are in our lives for a reason, season, and lifetime. We must learn which place each person in our lives must go. Even if things change, we must adjust with it.

There are times when you have been called to teach others, God will sit you down to teach you more. Then you can pour more into others. The way the world is set up some people will never visit my church, New Life SE, or even believe in my God. But when they hear and see what I went through and how God brought me out, I believe it will be some that will be moved by the power of God. See everything I went through, it was never about me. It was about the glory of God being revealed. God used a wretch like me and allowed me to be so sick so that He can show His power amongst His people who don't believe.

Remember no circumstance is beyond God's authority, nothing is too impossible for Him. Our problems, test, trials, storms, seasons of testing, whatever you might call it serves a purpose bigger than us. At times you might have to look weak to win. So that our latter will be greater, and we can have beauty before ashes. Remember Jesus said, "My disciples will do greater works." No matter how difficult the fight seems, keep fighting. Soon we will discover when we are with Jesus Christ, it was all worth it. The only fight God expects us to fight is the good fight of faith. I have learned about this thing called *redemptive suffering*. This is when you go through a problem or pain for the benefit of others. Never doubt in the dark what was told to you in the light. Everything Peter did and went through, at the end, his shadow alone healed many.

    I pray my journey and testimony has increased your faith tremendously, and that you see God above everything you are or will face. In the book of James, chapter two and verse one, God does not play favoritism, what He did for one He will do for another. He loves us all equally. Even though I know I am spoiled by God, He got you, too. But the Bible does say according to your faith so be it unto you. My crisis was a set up for the glory of God to be revealed. God needed it to go public because today many have lost faith in God. As you can see God never left me nor forsook me, I told you His word is true. God has launched me in 2017. Today I decree and declare in the mighty name of Jesus that, I've Been Released!!! Now it's time for me to live my God-given purpose.

Conclusion

Jeremiah 1:5 says, "before I formed thee in the belly I knew thee, and before thou camest forth out of the womb I sanctified thee, and I ordained thee a prophet unto the nations." Then a little further in the book of Jeremiah 29:11 it states, "for I know the thoughts I think toward you, saith the Lord, thoughts of peace and not of evil, to give you an expected end."

Now let's look in the middle. God knew you before He formed you and everything you have endured have been predestined. Our journeys depend on our obedience towards God's word. There are blessings for obedience and curses for disobedience. His laws and word is set in place to protect us from dangers. But when we break them, He is still God, and when we repent, He comes and saves the day. Glory to God!!!!

As Christians, we are not promised that no suffering or calamities will come our way - especially when we are disobedient as I were early in my life. God expects us during those times to express our faith to the world. As long as God, who knows our future, provides our plan and be with us as we fulfill our purpose, we can have unlimited faith in Him. Faith releases God's power. God only asks that we as His children only have faith the size of a mustard seed. Wow! God doesn't ask for much, yet give so much in return.

Even through our pain, suffering, and hardships, God will see us through to a glorious conclusion. God is ready to release you. Are you ready to trust Him? Out of all the hell and heartaches and disappointments you have experienced God allowed it for your preparation. Rather self-inflicted or not, God still has you in mind to do something wonderful here on earth. I dare you to step out in faith in God.

Those things that had you bound, and the plan and purpose God has for your life, through them you begin to see the hand of God in them. This is when you, too, can testify that, I've Been Released.

My prayer is that this book has inspired, encouraged you, and has provided you with the wisdom and knowledge and boldness that you needed from God to go forth. I pray that the spirit of fear be broken off your life so that the plan and will of God for your life can go forth. Keep believing in God. Keep seeking God, and remember to love on God like never before.

Don't let it stop here. Prayerfully someone has been released from strongholds, church hurt, generational curses, rejection, abandonment, unworthiness, doubt and fear, and low self-esteem. If you believe God has released you, as I know He will if you only believe, from any or all of these things then spread the word. Tell someone else about the goodness of God and all He has done for us. Together let's glorify our great, powerful, matchless God. So that others can testify, I've Been Released!!! Doesn't it feel good to be released?

This book is dedicated to my Lord and Savior, Jesus Christ, my mighty and strong and patient Counselor.

About the Author

Born as Nieta Shamone Sanson, the baby of four, truly put it all out there with this powerful, Spirit-led book. Nieta never desired to be an author, but truly felt obedient to follow God's plan with this book. She is currently a member of New Life SouthEast for seven years, under the Servant-leadership of Senior Pastor John F. Hannah. She has a heart of compassion for God's people. Nieta truly loves and adores her son, Demetrius, aka Turbo, who is now fourteen years old and is walking in his God-given talent. Turbo is looking to further his basketball skills all the way to the NBA. Still encouraged daily by her son, Nieta covers her son in prayer believing that God will not allow him to fall in the many pit holes she fell in. God allows Nieta to see where people are and encourage them to be all God created them to be. She often believes in others even when they don't believe in themselves - just as God did her.

Nieta's magnetic personality and warm smile draws many towards her. God has truly brought her from a mighty long way. Back in the day, she walked around daily with a frown on her face – but God turned it into a smile. One of Nieta's prayers is that she touches and helps change the life of at least just one young lady. Hoping to lead her to God and help her to learn her worth and value, and not go down the path she endured. If one listens and follows, then it would make it all worth it.

Nieta has been certified to work in the medical field for over thirteen years now, but that is not where her passion lies. She is now a certified Spiritual Empowerment Life Coach and is continuing in the position of founder and director of Release Dance Ministry. A job she is excited to govern because watching God change the lives of others right before her eyes is priceless. Nieta is continuing her education in behavioral science. She has been blessed to start a powerful new business, D.E.B.O.R.A.H Empowerment Life Coach Industry.

Another thing that brings joy to Nieta's life is serving God's people in any way she can. She serves in multiple ministries at her church. She treats everyone that comes in her path like VIP. She's still believing God to send her Boaz. She believes that 2017 was the beginning of restoration for her and her son. She cannot wait to share that testimony with the world. She has been inspired by God to write more books, so spread the word and keep your eyes and ears open for more.

Nieta Shamone Ministries 708-595-0462

Nieta Shamone - Chief Experience Officer

Author/Motivational Speaker Facebook: Nieta Shamone Ministries

Email NietaShamoneministries@yahoo.com

D.E.B.O.R.A.H Empowerment Life Coach Industry

Release Dance Ministry. Founder and CEO

www.ingramcontent.com/pod-product-compliance
Lightning Source LLC
Chambersburg PA
CBHW070321100426
42743CB00011B/2511